Somerset Trig Bagger

Trig points, or trigonometrical stations to give
common sight and much-loved feature of Brita
1962 as part of the Ordnance Survey's Retriangu _.., tnis log book
is your ideal hiking companion as you 'bag' them. ... oomerset

Keeping a logbook is great for reminiscing about your adventures, share your hikes
with friends and family - tick off the list as you complete the challenges one by one.
This log book contains 112 trig pillars in Somerset, so get your hiking boots on and
take on the Somerset Trigs Challenge!

How to use this logbook...

Use the map page to select the trig you are
planning to visit, then identify them in the
contents page.

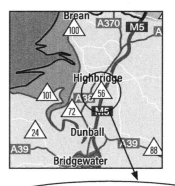

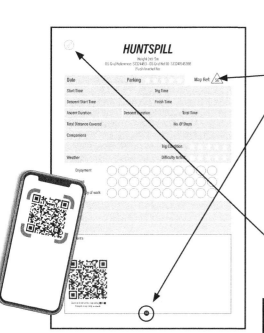

56 HUNTSPILL

Go to the logbook page, then scan
the QR code to open a map on your
smartphone so you can plan your
route. Note the OS grid reference
which you can enter into your GPS
to follow on the day.

Record your adventure
and tick off the trig when
you're done!

TOP TIP:
You can zoom in and out on the map on your phone
by pressing the ⊞ and ⊟ buttons. Take screenhots
in case you are out of mobile data on the hills!

Trig Finder - *At a glance*

1	ASHTON HILL	40	DEANS CROSS	79	PLANTATION FARM
2	BAGBOROUGH	41	DEVILS PUNCH BOWL	80	POSTLEBURY
3	BAGGRIDGE FARM	42	DIAL HILL	81	POTTERSHILL
4	BAGLEY RESR	43	DOULTING	82	PYNCOMBE FARM
5	BANNERDOWN	44	DUNCORN HILL	83	RAINBOW WOOD
6	BARRINGTON HILL	45	DUNDRY	84	REDLYNCH
7	BATHAMPTON DOWN	46	EAKER HILL	85	ROCK
8	BEACON HILL	47	EDGEBOROUGH	86	RYDON HILL
9	BEN KNOWLE HILL	48	ELSWORTHY	87	SELWORTHY BEACON
10	BLACK HILL	49	FROME RESR	88	SHAPWICK
11	BLACKBERRY HILL	50	GREAT NURCOTT	89	SMALL DOWN KNOLL
12	BLAGDON	51	HADDON BEACON	90	SNOWDON HILL
13	BLAGDON HILL	52	HERNE HILL	91	SOLSBURY HILL
14	BRATTON HILL	53	HIGHER WHITEFIELD FARM	92	ST RAYN HILL
15	BREACH HILL	54	HOME FARM	93	STAPLE HILL
16	BREAN DOWN	55	HONEYGAR	94	STEEP HOLME
17	BROMPTON RALPH	56	HUNTSPILL	95	STOCKLINCH
18	BROOMFIELD HILL	57	KELSTON ROUND HILL	96	STOKE HILL
19	BUCKLAND HILL	58	KINGS	97	STORRIDGE HILL
20	BURLEDGE HILL	59	KINGSDON HILL	98	TREBOROUGH COMMON
21	BURROW HILL	60	LEIGH FARM	99	TWERTON HILL
22	BUTSONS	61	LOLLOVER HILL	100	UNITY FARM
23	CAMEL HILL	62	LOXTON HILL	101	WALL COMMON
24	CANNINGTON PARK	63	LYPE HILL	102	WARREN FARM
25	CASTLE CARY RESR	64	MAES KNOLL	103	WAVERING DOWN
26	CHAINS BARROW	65	MENDIP GOLF LINKS	104	WESTBURY BEACON
27	CHAPEL LEIGH	66	MERRIDGE	105	WESTON
28	CHAPEL PILL FARM	67	MIDDLE HOPE	106	WINDMILL FARM
29	CHARLTON HILL	68	NEW PLANTATION	107	WINDMILL HILL RESR
30	CHIBBET CROSS	69	NORTH HILL	108	WINSFORD HILL
31	CHINNOCK HILL	70	NYLAND HILL	109	WITHYPOOL COMMON
32	COKER HILL	71	PAULTON	110	WOODFORD
33	COMBE BEACON	72	PAWLETT	111	WRAXALL
34	CORTON HILL	73	PEN HILL	112	YANLEY
35	COURT DOWN	74	PENNARD HILL		
36	CREECH HILL	75	PENSELWOOD		
37	CROYDON HILL	76	PERRITON HILL		
38	CULBONE HILL	77	PILTON		
39	DAWS GREEN	78	PINNACLE HILL		

Trig Finder

At a glance...

Scan QR code to open this map on your phone or tablet.

Trig Tick Offs - In Alphabetical Order

Trig Finder - In Height Ascending Order

ASHTON HILL

Height (m): 116m
OS Grid Reference: ST675653 · OS Grid Ref 10: ST6753265390
Flush bracket No: S2400

Date	Parking ☆☆☆☆☆	Map Ref: △ 1

Start Time	Trig Time

Descent Start Time	Finish Time

Ascent Duration	Descent Duration	Total Time

Total Distance Covered	No. Of Steps

Companions

	Trig Condition ☆☆☆☆☆

Weather	Difficulty to find ☆☆☆☆☆

Enjoyment	○ ○ ○ ○ ○ ○ ○ ○ ○ ○
Views	○ ○ ○ ○ ○ ○ ○ ○ ○ ○
Difficulty of walk	○ ○ ○ ○ ○ ○ ○ ○ ○ ○

Highlights

Comments

Zoom in & out on the map using ➕ & ➖
Navigate map using ▲ ◀ ▼ ▶

BAGBOROUGH

Height (m): 385m
OS Grid Reference: ST165351 • OS Grid Ref 10: ST1653235155
Flush bracket No: S1526

Date	Parking ★ ★ ★ ★ ★	Map Ref: △ 2

Start Time	Trig Time

Descent Start Time	Finish Time

Ascent Duration	Descent Duration	Total Time

Total Distance Covered	No. Of Steps

Companions

	Trig Condition ★ ★ ★ ★ ★

Weather	Difficulty to find ★ ★ ★ ★ ★

Enjoyment ○ ○ ○ ○ ○ ○ ○ ○ ○ ○

Views ○ ○ ○ ○ ○ ○ ○ ○ ○ ○

Difficulty of walk ○ ○ ○ ○ ○ ○ ○ ○ ○ ○

Highlights

Comments

Zoom in & out on the map using ➕ & ➖
Navigate map using ▲ ◀ ▼ ▶

BAGGRIDGE FARM

Height (m): 157m
OS Grid Reference: ST744567 · OS Grid Ref 10: ST7449556707
Flush bracket No: S2485

Date		Parking ★★★★★		Map Ref: 3
Start Time		Trig Time		
Descent Start Time		Finish Time		
Ascent Duration	Descent Duration		Total Time	
Total Distance Covered			No. Of Steps	
Companions				
		Trig Condition ★★★★★		
Weather		Difficulty to find ★★★★★		

Enjoyment ○ ○ ○ ○ ○ ○ ○ ○ ○ ○

Views ○ ○ ○ ○ ○ ○ ○ ○ ○ ○

Difficulty of walk ○ ○ ○ ○ ○ ○ ○ ○ ○ ○

Highlights

Comments

Zoom in & out on the map using ➕ & ➖
Navigate map using ▲ ◀ ▼ ▶

BAGLEY RESR

Height (m): 72m
OS Grid Reference: ST449459 • OS Grid Ref 10: ST4497945966
Flush bracket No: S3246

Date	Parking ★ ★ ★ ★ ★	Map Ref: △ 4

Start Time	Trig Time

Descent Start Time	Finish Time

Ascent Duration	Descent Duration	Total Time

Total Distance Covered	No. Of Steps

Companions

	Trig Condition ★ ★ ★ ★ ★

Weather	Difficulty to find ★ ★ ★ ★ ★

Enjoyment ◯ ◯ ◯ ◯ ◯ ◯ ◯ ◯ ◯ ◯

Views ◯ ◯ ◯ ◯ ◯ ◯ ◯ ◯ ◯ ◯

Difficulty of walk ◯ ◯ ◯ ◯ ◯ ◯ ◯ ◯ ◯ ◯

Highlights

Comments

Zoom in & out on the map using ➕ & ➖
Navigate map using ▲ ◀ ▼ ▶

BANNERDOWN

Height (m): 183m
OS Grid Reference: ST792684 • OS Grid Ref 10: ST7922868434
Flush bracket No: S3220

Date	Parking ☆☆☆☆☆	Map Ref: △ 5

Start Time	Trig Time

Descent Start Time	Finish Time

Ascent Duration	Descent Duration	Total Time

Total Distance Covered	No. Of Steps

Companions

Trig Condition ☆☆☆☆☆

Weather | Difficulty to find ☆☆☆☆☆

Enjoyment ○○○○○○○○○○

Views ○○○○○○○○○○

Difficulty of walk ○○○○○○○○○○

Highlights

Comments

Zoom in & out on the map using ➕ & ➖
Navigate map using ▲ ◀ ▼ ▶

BARRINGTON HILL

Height (m): 102m
OS Grid Reference: ST295170 · OS Grid Ref 10: ST2953517052
Flush bracket No: S3740

Date	Parking ★ ★ ★ ★ ★	Map Ref: △6

Start Time	Trig Time

Descent Start Time	Finish Time

Ascent Duration	Descent Duration	Total Time

Total Distance Covered	No. Of Steps

Companions

	Trig Condition ★ ★ ★ ★ ★

Weather	Difficulty to find ★ ★ ★ ★ ★

Enjoyment ○ ○ ○ ○ ○ ○ ○ ○ ○ ○

Views ○ ○ ○ ○ ○ ○ ○ ○ ○ ○

Difficulty of walk ○ ○ ○ ○ ○ ○ ○ ○ ○ ○

Highlights

Comments

Zoom in & out on the map using ➕ & ➖
Navigate map using ▲ ◀ ▼ ▶

BATHAMPTON DOWN

Height (m): 204m
OS Grid Reference: ST773651 · OS Grid Ref 10: ST7736565107
Flush bracket No: S3228

Date	Parking ⭐⭐⭐⭐⭐	Map Ref: △ 7

Start Time	Trig Time

Descent Start Time	Finish Time

Ascent Duration	Descent Duration	Total Time

Total Distance Covered	No. Of Steps

Companions

Trig Condition ⭐⭐⭐⭐⭐

Weather	Difficulty to find ⭐⭐⭐⭐⭐

Enjoyment ◯◯◯◯◯◯◯◯◯◯

Views ◯◯◯◯◯◯◯◯◯◯

Difficulty of walk ◯◯◯◯◯◯◯◯◯◯

Highlights

Comments

Zoom in & out on the map using ➕ & ➖
Navigate map using ▲ ◀ ▼ ▶

BEACON HILL

Height (m): 311m
OS Grid Reference: ST124409 · OS Grid Ref 10: ST1245240994
Flush bracket No: S3757

Date	Parking ★ ★ ★ ★ ★	Map Ref: △ 8

Start Time	Trig Time

Descent Start Time	Finish Time

Ascent Duration	Descent Duration	Total Time

Total Distance Covered	No. Of Steps

Companions

Trig Condition ★ ★ ★ ★ ★

Weather | Difficulty to find ★ ★ ★ ★ ★

Enjoyment ◯ ◯ ◯ ◯ ◯ ◯ ◯ ◯ ◯ ◯

Views ◯ ◯ ◯ ◯ ◯ ◯ ◯ ◯ ◯ ◯

Difficulty of walk ◯ ◯ ◯ ◯ ◯ ◯ ◯ ◯ ◯ ◯

Highlights

Comments

Zoom in & out on the map using ➕ & ➖
Navigate map using ▲ ◀ ▼ ▶

BEN KNOWLE HILL

Height (m): 99m
OS Grid Reference: ST516448 · OS Grid Ref 10: ST5162944899
Flush bracket No: S3254

Date	Parking ★★★★★★	Map Ref: △ 9

Start Time	Trig Time

Descent Start Time	Finish Time

Ascent Duration	Descent Duration	Total Time

Total Distance Covered	No. Of Steps

Companions	

	Trig Condition ★★★★★

Weather	Difficulty to find ★★★★★

Enjoyment ○○○○○○○○○

Views ○○○○○○○○○

Difficulty of walk ○○○○○○○○○

Highlights

Comments

Zoom in & out on the map using ➕ & ➖
Navigate map using ▲ ◀ ▼ ▶

BLACK HILL

Height (m): 358m
OS Grid Reference: ST148380 · OS Grid Ref 10: ST1481838098
Flush bracket No: S3750

Date	Parking ★ ★ ★ ★ ★	Map Ref: △ 10

Start Time	Trig Time

Descent Start Time	Finish Time

Ascent Duration	Descent Duration	Total Time

Total Distance Covered	No. Of Steps

Companions

	Trig Condition ★ ★ ★ ★ ★

Weather	Difficulty to find ★ ★ ★ ★ ★

Enjoyment ○ ○ ○ ○ ○ ○ ○ ○ ○ ○

Views ○ ○ ○ ○ ○ ○ ○ ○ ○ ○

Difficulty of walk ○ ○ ○ ○ ○ ○ ○ ○ ○ ○

Highlights

Comments

Zoom in & out on the map using ➕ & ➖
Navigate map using ▲ ◀ ▼ ▶

BLACKBERRY HILL

Height (m): 208m
OS Grid Reference: ST639601 · OS Grid Ref 10: ST6399760161
Flush bracket No: S2556

| Date | Parking ☆☆☆☆☆ | Map Ref: △ 11 |

Start Time | Trig Time

Descent Start Time | Finish Time

Ascent Duration | Descent Duration | Total Time

Total Distance Covered | No. Of Steps

Companions

Trig Condition ☆☆☆☆☆

Weather | Difficulty to find ☆☆☆☆☆

Enjoyment ○○○○○○○○○○
Views ○○○○○○○○○○
Difficulty of walk ○○○○○○○○○○

Highlights

Comments

Zoom in & out on the map using ➕ & ➖
Navigate map using ▲ ◀ ▼ ▶

11

BLAGDON

Height (m): 325m
OS Grid Reference: ST484572 · OS Grid Ref 10: ST4846157265
Flush bracket No: S1516

Date	Parking ★ ★ ★ ★ ★	Map Ref: 12

Start Time	Trig Time

Descent Start Time	Finish Time

Ascent Duration	Descent Duration	Total Time

Total Distance Covered	No. Of Steps

Companions	

	Trig Condition ★ ★ ★ ★ ★

Weather	Difficulty to find ★ ★ ★ ★ ★

Enjoyment ◯ ◯ ◯ ◯ ◯ ◯ ◯ ◯ ◯ ◯

Views ◯ ◯ ◯ ◯ ◯ ◯ ◯ ◯ ◯ ◯

Difficulty of walk ◯ ◯ ◯ ◯ ◯ ◯ ◯ ◯ ◯ ◯

Highlights

Comments

Zoom in & out on the map using ➕ & ➖
Navigate map using ▲ ◀ ▼ ▶

BLAGDON HILL

Height (m): 361m
OS Grid Reference: SS971337 • OS Grid Ref 10: SS9712233749
Flush bracket No: S3924

Date	Parking	Map Ref: /13\

Start Time | **Trig Time**

Descent Start Time | **Finish Time**

Ascent Duration | **Descent Duration** | **Total Time**

Total Distance Covered | **No. Of Steps**

Companions

Trig Condition ⭐⭐⭐⭐⭐

Weather | **Difficulty to find** ⭐⭐⭐⭐⭐

Enjoyment ◯◯◯◯◯◯◯◯◯◯

Views ◯◯◯◯◯◯◯◯◯◯

Difficulty of walk ◯◯◯◯◯◯◯◯◯◯

Highlights

Comments

Zoom in & out on the map using ➕ & ➖
Navigate map using ▲ ◀ ▼ ▶

BRATTON HILL

Height (m): 184m
OS Grid Reference: ST673296 · OS Grid Ref 10: ST6734629679
Flush bracket No: S5145

Date	Parking ★ ★ ★ ★ ★	Map Ref: 14

Start Time	Trig Time

Descent Start Time	Finish Time

Ascent Duration	Descent Duration	Total Time

Total Distance Covered	No. Of Steps

Companions

	Trig Condition ★ ★ ★ ★ ★

Weather	Difficulty to find ★ ★ ★ ★ ★

Enjoyment	○ ○ ○ ○ ○ ○ ○ ○ ○ ○
Views	○ ○ ○ ○ ○ ○ ○ ○ ○ ○
Difficulty of walk	○ ○ ○ ○ ○ ○ ○ ○ ○ ○

Highlights

Comments

Zoom in & out on the map using ⊞ & ⊟
Navigate map using ▲ ◀ ▼ ▶

BREACH HILL

Height (m): 133m
OS Grid Reference: ST545601 · OS Grid Ref 10: ST5457160133
Flush bracket No: S3263

Date	Parking ★★★★★	Map Ref: /15\

Start Time	Trig Time

Descent Start Time	Finish Time

Ascent Duration	Descent Duration	Total Time

Total Distance Covered	No. Of Steps

Companions

	Trig Condition ★★★★★

Weather	Difficulty to find ★★★★★

Enjoyment ○○○○○○○○○○

Views ○○○○○○○○○○

Difficulty of walk ○○○○○○○○○○

Highlights

Comments

Zoom in & out on the map using ➕ & ➖
Navigate map using ▲ ◀ ▼ ▶

BREAN DOWN

Height (m): 98m
OS Grid Reference: ST284590 · OS Grid Ref 10: ST2849159007
Flush bracket No: S3270

Date	Parking ★ ★ ★ ★ ★	Map Ref: △16

Start Time | **Trig Time**

Descent Start Time | **Finish Time**

Ascent Duration | **Descent Duration** | **Total Time**

Total Distance Covered | **No. Of Steps**

Companions

Trig Condition ★ ★ ★ ★ ★

Weather | **Difficulty to find** ★ ★ ★ ★ ★

Enjoyment ○ ○ ○ ○ ○ ○ ○ ○ ○ ○

Views ○ ○ ○ ○ ○ ○ ○ ○ ○ ○

Difficulty of walk ○ ○ ○ ○ ○ ○ ○ ○ ○ ○

Highlights

Comments

Zoom in & out on the map using ➕ & ➖
Navigate map using ▲ ◀ ▼ ▶

BROMPTON RALPH

Height (m): 393m
OS Grid Reference: ST071338 · OS Grid Ref 10: ST0711333819
Flush bracket No: S3737

Date	Parking ★★★★★	Map Ref: /17\

Start Time	Trig Time

Descent Start Time	Finish Time

Ascent Duration	Descent Duration	Total Time

Total Distance Covered	No. Of Steps

Companions

Trig Condition ★★★★★

Weather	Difficulty to find ★★★★★

Enjoyment ○ ○ ○ ○ ○ ○ ○ ○ ○ ○

Views ○ ○ ○ ○ ○ ○ ○ ○ ○ ○

Difficulty of walk ○ ○ ○ ○ ○ ○ ○ ○ ○ ○

Highlights

Comments

Zoom in & out on the map using ➕ & ➖
Navigate map using ▲ ◀ ▼ ▶

BROOMFIELD HILL

Height (m): 291m
OS Grid Reference: ST215331 • OS Grid Ref 10: ST2154333190
Flush bracket No: S3735

Date	Parking ★ ★ ★ ★ ★	Map Ref: △ 18

Start Time	Trig Time

Descent Start Time	Finish Time

Ascent Duration	Descent Duration	Total Time

Total Distance Covered	No. Of Steps

Companions

Trig Condition ★ ★ ★ ★ ★

Weather	Difficulty to find ★ ★ ★ ★ ★

Enjoyment	◯ ◯ ◯ ◯ ◯ ◯ ◯ ◯ ◯ ◯
Views	◯ ◯ ◯ ◯ ◯ ◯ ◯ ◯ ◯ ◯
Difficulty of walk	◯ ◯ ◯ ◯ ◯ ◯ ◯ ◯ ◯ ◯

Highlights

Comments

Zoom in & out on the map using ➕ & ➖
Navigate map using ▲ ◀ ▼ ▶

BUCKLAND HILL

Height (m): 281m
OS Grid Reference: ST166176 · OS Grid Ref 10: ST1669217648
Flush bracket No: S3776

Date	Parking ★★★★★	Map Ref: /19\

Start Time	Trig Time

Descent Start Time	Finish Time

Ascent Duration	Descent Duration	Total Time

Total Distance Covered	No. Of Steps

Companions

	Trig Condition ★★★★★

Weather	Difficulty to find ★★★★★

Enjoyment ○○○○○○○○○○

Views ○○○○○○○○○○

Difficulty of walk ○○○○○○○○○○

Highlights

Comments

Zoom in & out on the map using ➕ & ➖
Navigate map using ▲ ◀ ▼ ▶

BURLEDGE HILL

Height (m): 174m
OS Grid Reference: ST588589 · OS Grid Ref 10: ST5883858904
Flush bracket No: S2552

Date	Parking ★★★★★	Map Ref: /20\

Start Time	Trig Time

Descent Start Time	Finish Time

Ascent Duration	Descent Duration	Total Time

Total Distance Covered	No. Of Steps

Companions

Trig Condition ★★★★★

Weather	Difficulty to find ★★★★★

Enjoyment ○○○○○○○○○○

Views ○○○○○○○○○○

Difficulty of walk ○○○○○○○○○○

Highlights

Comments

Zoom in & out on the map using ➕ & ➖
Navigate map using ▲ ◀ ▼ ▶

BURROW HILL

Height (m): 78m
OS Grid Reference: ST414201 • OS Grid Ref 10: ST4144720116
Flush bracket No: S5896

Date	Parking ★★★★★	Map Ref: /21\

Start Time	Trig Time

Descent Start Time	Finish Time

Ascent Duration	Descent Duration	Total Time

Total Distance Covered	No. Of Steps

Companions

Trig Condition ★★★★★

Weather | Difficulty to find ★★★★★

Enjoyment ○○○○○○○○○○
Views ○○○○○○○○○○
Difficulty of walk ○○○○○○○○○○

Highlights

Comments

Zoom in & out on the map using ➕ & ➖
Navigate map using ▲ ◀ ▼ ▶

BUTSONS

Height (m): 139m
OS Grid Reference: SS909355 • OS Grid Ref 10: SS9096835584
Flush bracket No: S3773

Date	Parking ★ ★ ★ ★ ★	Map Ref: /22\

Start Time	Trig Time

Descent Start Time	Finish Time

Ascent Duration	Descent Duration	Total Time

Total Distance Covered	No. Of Steps

Companions

	Trig Condition ★ ★ ★ ★ ★

Weather	Difficulty to find ★ ★ ★ ★ ★

Enjoyment ○ ○ ○ ○ ○ ○ ○ ○ ○ ○

Views ○ ○ ○ ○ ○ ○ ○ ○ ○ ○

Difficulty of walk ○ ○ ○ ○ ○ ○ ○ ○ ○ ○

Highlights

Comments

Zoom in & out on the map using ➕ & ➖
Navigate map using ▲ ◀ ▼ ▶

CAMEL HILL

Height (m): 80m
OS Grid Reference: ST592255 · OS Grid Ref 10: ST5922925506
Flush bracket No: S5887

Date	Parking ★★★★★	Map Ref: /23\

Start Time	Trig Time

Descent Start Time	Finish Time

Ascent Duration	Descent Duration	Total Time

Total Distance Covered	No. Of Steps

Companions	

	Trig Condition ★★★★★

Weather	Difficulty to find ★★★★★

Enjoyment	○ ○ ○ ○ ○ ○ ○ ○ ○ ○
Views	○ ○ ○ ○ ○ ○ ○ ○ ○ ○
Difficulty of walk	○ ○ ○ ○ ○ ○ ○ ○ ○ ○

Highlights

Comments

Zoom in & out on the map using ➕ & ➖
Navigate map using ▲ ◀ ▼ ▶

CANNINGTON PARK

Height (m): 80m
OS Grid Reference: ST246404 • OS Grid Ref 10: ST2461440464
Flush bracket No: S3252

Date	Parking ★★★★★	Map Ref: △24

Start Time	Trig Time

Descent Start Time	Finish Time

Ascent Duration	Descent Duration	Total Time

Total Distance Covered	No. Of Steps

Companions

	Trig Condition ★★★★★

Weather	Difficulty to find ★★★★★

Enjoyment ○○○○○○○○○○

Views ○○○○○○○○○○

Difficulty of walk ○○○○○○○○○○

Highlights

Comments

Zoom in & out on the map using ➕ & ➖
Navigate map using ▲ ◀ ▼ ▶

CASTLE CARY RESR

Height (m): 155m
OS Grid Reference: ST643317 • OS Grid Ref 10: ST6431031718
Flush bracket No: S5877

Date	Parking ★★★★★	Map Ref: /25\

Start Time	Trig Time

Descent Start Time	Finish Time

Ascent Duration	Descent Duration	Total Time

Total Distance Covered	No. Of Steps

Companions	

	Trig Condition ★★★★★

Weather	Difficulty to find ★★★★★

Enjoyment ○ ○ ○ ○ ○ ○ ○ ○ ○ ○

Views ○ ○ ○ ○ ○ ○ ○ ○ ○ ○

Difficulty of walk ○ ○ ○ ○ ○ ○ ○ ○ ○ ○

Highlights

Comments

Zoom in & out on the map using ➕ & ➖
Navigate map using ▲ ◀ ▼ ▶

CHAINS BARROW

Height (m): 488m
OS Grid Reference: SS734419 · OS Grid Ref 10: SS7345741904
Flush bracket No: S5166

Date	Parking ★ ★ ★ ★ ★	Map Ref: △26

Start Time	Trig Time

Descent Start Time	Finish Time

Ascent Duration	Descent Duration	Total Time

Total Distance Covered	No. Of Steps

Companions

	Trig Condition ★ ★ ★ ★ ★

Weather	Difficulty to find ★ ★ ★ ★ ★

Enjoyment ○ ○ ○ ○ ○ ○ ○ ○ ○ ○

Views ○ ○ ○ ○ ○ ○ ○ ○ ○ ○

Difficulty of walk ○ ○ ○ ○ ○ ○ ○ ○ ○ ○

Highlights

Comments

Zoom in & out on the map using ➕ & ➖
Navigate map using ▲ ◄ ▼ ►

CHAPEL LEIGH

Height (m): 169m
OS Grid Reference: ST132299 · OS Grid Ref 10: ST1324229914
Flush bracket No: S3731

Date	Parking ⭐⭐⭐⭐⭐	Map Ref: /27\

Start Time	Trig Time

Descent Start Time	Finish Time

Ascent Duration	Descent Duration	Total Time

Total Distance Covered	No. Of Steps

Companions

	Trig Condition ⭐⭐⭐⭐⭐

Weather	Difficulty to find ⭐⭐⭐⭐⭐

Enjoyment ○ ○ ○ ○ ○ ○ ○ ○ ○ ○

Views ○ ○ ○ ○ ○ ○ ○ ○ ○ ○

Difficulty of walk ○ ○ ○ ○ ○ ○ ○ ○ ○ ○

Highlights

Comments

Zoom in & out on the map using ➕ & ➖
Navigate map using ▲ ◀ ▼ ▶

CHAPEL PILL FARM

Height (m): 31m
OS Grid Reference: ST539759 · OS Grid Ref 10: ST5396275903
Flush bracket No: S3375

Date	Parking ★ ★ ★ ★ ★	Map Ref: /28\

Start Time	Trig Time

Descent Start Time	Finish Time

Ascent Duration	Descent Duration	Total Time

Total Distance Covered	No. Of Steps

Companions

	Trig Condition ★ ★ ★ ★ ★

Weather	Difficulty to find ★ ★ ★ ★ ★

Enjoyment ◯ ◯ ◯ ◯ ◯ ◯ ◯ ◯ ◯ ◯

Views ◯ ◯ ◯ ◯ ◯ ◯ ◯ ◯ ◯ ◯

Difficulty of walk ◯ ◯ ◯ ◯ ◯ ◯ ◯ ◯ ◯ ◯

Highlights

Comments

Zoom in & out on the map using ➕ & ➖
Navigate map using ▲ ◀ ▼ ▶

CHARLTON HILL

Height (m): 183m
OS Grid Reference: ST671242 • OS Grid Ref 10: ST6717324220
Flush bracket No: S5713

Date	Parking ⭐⭐⭐⭐⭐	Map Ref: /29\

Start Time	Trig Time

Descent Start Time	Finish Time

Ascent Duration	Descent Duration	Total Time

Total Distance Covered	No. Of Steps

Companions

	Trig Condition ⭐⭐⭐⭐⭐

Weather	Difficulty to find ⭐⭐⭐⭐⭐

Enjoyment ○ ○ ○ ○ ○ ○ ○ ○ ○ ○

Views ○ ○ ○ ○ ○ ○ ○ ○ ○ ○

Difficulty of walk ○ ○ ○ ○ ○ ○ ○ ○ ○ ○

Highlights

Comments

Zoom in & out on the map using ➕ & ➖
Navigate map using ▲ ◀ ▼ ▶

CHIBBET CROSS

Height (m): 392m
OS Grid Reference: SS852370 • OS Grid Ref 10: SS8522537026
Flush bracket No: S5440

Date	Parking ★ ★ ★ ★ ★	Map Ref: △30

Start Time	Trig Time

Descent Start Time	Finish Time

Ascent Duration	Descent Duration	Total Time

Total Distance Covered	No. Of Steps

Companions

	Trig Condition ★ ★ ★ ★ ★

Weather	Difficulty to find ★ ★ ★ ★ ★

Enjoyment ○ ○ ○ ○ ○ ○ ○ ○ ○ ○

Views ○ ○ ○ ○ ○ ○ ○ ○ ○ ○

Difficulty of walk ○ ○ ○ ○ ○ ○ ○ ○ ○ ○

Highlights

Comments

Zoom in & out on the map using ➕ & ➖
Navigate map using ▲ ◀ ▼ ▶

CHINNOCK HILL

Height (m): 78m
OS Grid Reference: ST461127 · OS Grid Ref 10: ST4612412771
Flush bracket No: S5894

Date	Parking ★★★★★	Map Ref: /31\

Start Time	Trig Time

Descent Start Time	Finish Time

Ascent Duration	Descent Duration	Total Time

Total Distance Covered	No. Of Steps

Companions

	Trig Condition ★★★★★

Weather	Difficulty to find ★★★★★

Enjoyment ○○○○○○○○○○

Views ○○○○○○○○○○

Difficulty of walk ○○○○○○○○○○

Highlights

Comments

Zoom in & out on the map using ➕ & ➖
Navigate map using ▲ ◀ ▼ ▶

COKER HILL

Height (m): 135m
OS Grid Reference: ST509132 · OS Grid Ref 10: ST5093613248
Flush bracket No: S6077

Date	Parking ★ ★ ★ ★ ★	Map Ref: /32\

Start Time	Trig Time

Descent Start Time	Finish Time

Ascent Duration	Descent Duration	Total Time

Total Distance Covered	No. Of Steps

Companions	

	Trig Condition ★ ★ ★ ★ ★

Weather	Difficulty to find ★ ★ ★ ★ ★

Enjoyment ○ ○ ○ ○ ○ ○ ○ ○ ○ ○

Views ○ ○ ○ ○ ○ ○ ○ ○ ○ ○

Difficulty of walk ○ ○ ○ ○ ○ ○ ○ ○ ○ ○

Highlights

Comments

Zoom in & out on the map using ➕ & ➖
Navigate map using ▲ ◀ ▼ ▶

COMBE BEACON

Height (m): 250m
OS Grid Reference: ST294122 · OS Grid Ref 10: ST2948612280
Flush bracket No: S3741

Date	Parking ★★★★★	Map Ref: /33\

Start Time	Trig Time

Descent Start Time	Finish Time

Ascent Duration	Descent Duration	Total Time

Total Distance Covered	No. Of Steps

Companions	

	Trig Condition ★★★★★

Weather	Difficulty to find ★★★★★

Enjoyment ○ ○ ○ ○ ○ ○ ○ ○ ○ ○

Views ○ ○ ○ ○ ○ ○ ○ ○ ○ ○

Difficulty of walk ○ ○ ○ ○ ○ ○ ○ ○ ○ ○

Highlights

Comments

Zoom in & out on the map using ➕ & ➖
Navigate map using ▲ ◀ ▼ ▶

CORTON HILL

Height (m): 197m
OS Grid Reference: ST632234 · OS Grid Ref 10: ST6328523413
Flush bracket No: S5875

Date	Parking ★ ★ ★ ★ ★	Map Ref: /34\

Start Time	Trig Time

Descent Start Time	Finish Time

Ascent Duration	Descent Duration	Total Time

Total Distance Covered	No. Of Steps

Companions

	Trig Condition ★ ★ ★ ★ ★

Weather	Difficulty to find ★ ★ ★ ★ ★

Enjoyment ○ ○ ○ ○ ○ ○ ○ ○ ○ ○

Views ○ ○ ○ ○ ○ ○ ○ ○ ○ ○

Difficulty of walk ○ ○ ○ ○ ○ ○ ○ ○ ○ ○

Highlights

Comments

Zoom in & out on the map using ➕ & ➖
Navigate map using ▲ ◀ ▼ ▶

COURT DOWN

Height (m): 316m
OS Grid Reference: SS915297 · OS Grid Ref 10: SS9159229714
Flush bracket No: S3968

Date	Parking ⭐⭐⭐⭐⭐	Map Ref: /35\

Start Time	Trig Time

Descent Start Time	Finish Time

Ascent Duration	Descent Duration	Total Time

Total Distance Covered	No. Of Steps

Companions

Trig Condition ⭐⭐⭐⭐⭐

Weather | Difficulty to find ⭐⭐⭐⭐⭐

Enjoyment ◯ ◯ ◯ ◯ ◯ ◯ ◯ ◯ ◯ ◯

Views ◯ ◯ ◯ ◯ ◯ ◯ ◯ ◯ ◯ ◯

Difficulty of walk ◯ ◯ ◯ ◯ ◯ ◯ ◯ ◯ ◯ ◯

Highlights

Comments

Zoom in & out on the map using ➕ & ➖
Navigate map using ▲ ◀ ▼ ▶

CREECH HILL

Height (m): 200m
OS Grid Reference: ST666365 · OS Grid Ref 10: ST6663236577
Flush bracket No: S5695

Date	Parking ★ ★ ★ ★ ★	Map Ref: /36\

Start Time	Trig Time

Descent Start Time	Finish Time

Ascent Duration	Descent Duration	Total Time

Total Distance Covered	No. Of Steps

Companions

	Trig Condition ★ ★ ★ ★ ★

Weather	Difficulty to find ★ ★ ★ ★ ★

Enjoyment ○ ○ ○ ○ ○ ○ ○ ○ ○ ○

Views ○ ○ ○ ○ ○ ○ ○ ○ ○ ○

Difficulty of walk ○ ○ ○ ○ ○ ○ ○ ○ ○ ○

Highlights

Comments

Zoom in & out on the map using ➕ & ➖
Navigate map using ▲ ◀ ▼ ▶

CROYDON HILL

Height (m): 382m
OS Grid Reference: SS986394 · OS Grid Ref 10: SS9867239446
Flush bracket No: S3759

Date	Parking ★★★★★	Map Ref: /37\

Start Time	Trig Time

Descent Start Time	Finish Time

Ascent Duration	Descent Duration	Total Time

Total Distance Covered	No. Of Steps

Companions	

	Trig Condition ★★★★★

Weather	Difficulty to find ★★★★★

Enjoyment ○○○○○○○○○○

Views ○○○○○○○○○○

Difficulty of walk ○○○○○○○○○

Highlights

Comments

Zoom in & out on the map using ➕ & ➖
Navigate map using ▲ ◀ ▼ ▶

CULBONE HILL

Height (m): 434m
OS Grid Reference: SS837466 · OS Grid Ref 10: SS8377646636
Flush bracket No: S5433

Date	Parking ★ ★ ★ ★ ★	Map Ref: △38

Start Time	Trig Time

Descent Start Time	Finish Time

Ascent Duration	Descent Duration	Total Time

Total Distance Covered	No. Of Steps

Companions	

	Trig Condition ★ ★ ★ ★ ★

Weather	Difficulty to find ★ ★ ★ ★ ★

Enjoyment ○ ○ ○ ○ ○ ○ ○ ○ ○ ○

Views ○ ○ ○ ○ ○ ○ ○ ○ ○ ○

Difficulty of walk ○ ○ ○ ○ ○ ○ ○ ○ ○ ○

Highlights

Comments

Zoom in & out on the map using ➕ & ➖
Navigate map using ▲ ◀ ▼ ▶

38

DAWS GREEN

Height (m): 85m
OS Grid Reference: ST190216 · OS Grid Ref 10: ST1903021614
Flush bracket No: S3730

Date	Parking ★★★★★	Map Ref: /39\

Start Time	Trig Time

Descent Start Time	Finish Time

Ascent Duration	Descent Duration	Total Time

Total Distance Covered	No. Of Steps

Companions

Trig Condition ★★★★★

Weather	Difficulty to find ★★★★★

Enjoyment ○○○○○○○○○○

Views ○○○○○○○○○○

Difficulty of walk ○○○○○○○○○○

Highlights

Comments

Zoom in & out on the map using ➕ & ➖
Navigate map using ▲ ◀ ▼ ▶

DEANS CROSS

Height (m): 158m
OS Grid Reference: ST120337 • OS Grid Ref 10: ST1209033717
Flush bracket No: S3734

Date	Parking ★ ★ ★ ★ ★	Map Ref: /40\
Start Time	Trig Time	
Descent Start Time	Finish Time	
Ascent Duration	Descent Duration	Total Time
Total Distance Covered	No. Of Steps	
Companions		
	Trig Condition ★ ★ ★ ★ ★	
Weather	Difficulty to find ★ ★ ★ ★ ★	

Enjoyment	○	○	○	○	○	○	○	○	○	○
Views	○	○	○	○	○	○	○	○	○	○
Difficulty of walk	○	○	○	○	○	○	○	○	○	○

Highlights

Comments

Zoom in & out on the map using ➕ & ➖
Navigate map using ▲ ◀ ▼ ▶

DEVILS PUNCH BOWL

Height (m): 294m
OS Grid Reference: ST547536 · OS Grid Ref 10: ST5474953650
Flush bracket No: S3260

Date	Parking ★★★★★★	Map Ref: /41\

Start Time	Trig Time

Descent Start Time	Finish Time

Ascent Duration	Descent Duration	Total Time

Total Distance Covered	No. Of Steps

Companions

Trig Condition ★★★★★★

Weather	Difficulty to find ★★★★★★

Enjoyment ○○○○○○○○○○○

Views ○○○○○○○○○○○

Difficulty of walk ○○○○○○○○○○○

Highlights

Comments

Zoom in & out on the map using ➕ & ➖
Navigate map using ▲ ◀ ▼ ▶

DIAL HILL

Height (m): 90m
OS Grid Reference: ST407719 • OS Grid Ref 10: ST4077771957
Flush bracket No: S3275

Date	Parking ★ ★ ★ ★ ★	Map Ref: /42\

Start Time	Trig Time

Descent Start Time	Finish Time

Ascent Duration	Descent Duration	Total Time

Total Distance Covered	No. Of Steps

Companions

	Trig Condition ★ ★ ★ ★ ★

Weather	Difficulty to find ★ ★ ★ ★ ★

Enjoyment ○ ○ ○ ○ ○ ○ ○ ○ ○ ○

Views ○ ○ ○ ○ ○ ○ ○ ○ ○ ○

Difficulty of walk ○ ○ ○ ○ ○ ○ ○ ○ ○ ○

Highlights

Comments

Zoom in & out on the map using ➕ & ➖
Navigate map using ▲ ◀ ▼ ▶

DOULTING

Height (m): 215m
OS Grid Reference: ST638418 · OS Grid Ref 10: ST6380241875
Flush bracket No: S2546

Date	Parking ★★★★★	Map Ref: /43\

Start Time		Trig Time

Descent Start Time		Finish Time

Ascent Duration	Descent Duration	Total Time

Total Distance Covered		No. Of Steps

Companions

	Trig Condition ★★★★★

Weather	Difficulty to find ★★★★★

Enjoyment ○○○○○○○○○○

Views ○○○○○○○○○○

Difficulty of walk ○○○○○○○○○○

Highlights

Comments

Zoom in & out on the map using ✚ & ▬
Navigate map using ▲ ◀ ▼ ▶

43

DUNCORN HILL

Height (m): 178m
OS Grid Reference: ST723610 • OS Grid Ref 10: ST7235261036
Flush bracket No: S2401

Date	Parking ★ ★ ★ ★ ★	Map Ref: 44

Start Time	Trig Time

Descent Start Time	Finish Time

Ascent Duration	Descent Duration	Total Time

Total Distance Covered	No. Of Steps

Companions

	Trig Condition ★ ★ ★ ★ ★

Weather	Difficulty to find ★ ★ ★ ★ ★

Enjoyment ◯ ◯ ◯ ◯ ◯ ◯ ◯ ◯ ◯ ◯

Views ◯ ◯ ◯ ◯ ◯ ◯ ◯ ◯ ◯ ◯

Difficulty of walk ◯ ◯ ◯ ◯ ◯ ◯ ◯ ◯ ◯ ◯

Highlights

Comments

Zoom in & out on the map using 🔼 & 🔽
Navigate map using ▲ ◀ ▼ ▶

DUNDRY

Height (m): 233m
OS Grid Reference: ST553667 · OS Grid Ref 10: ST5533866719
Flush bracket No: S3267

Date	Parking ☆☆☆☆☆	Map Ref: 45

Start Time	Trig Time

Descent Start Time	Finish Time

Ascent Duration	Descent Duration	Total Time

Total Distance Covered	No. Of Steps

Companions

	Trig Condition ☆☆☆☆☆

Weather	Difficulty to find ☆☆☆☆☆

Enjoyment ○○○○○○○○○○

Views ○○○○○○○○○○

Difficulty of walk ○○○○○○○○○○

Highlights

Comments

Zoom in & out on the map using ➕ & ➖
Navigate map using ▲ ◀ ▼ ▶

EAKER HILL

Height (m): 290m
OS Grid Reference: ST567523 • OS Grid Ref 10: ST5679952325
Flush bracket No: S2544

Date	Parking ★ ★ ★ ★ ★	Map Ref: /46\

Start Time	Trig Time

Descent Start Time	Finish Time

Ascent Duration	Descent Duration	Total Time

Total Distance Covered	No. Of Steps

Companions

	Trig Condition ★ ★ ★ ★ ★

Weather	Difficulty to find ★ ★ ★ ★ ★

Enjoyment ○ ○ ○ ○ ○ ○ ○ ○ ○ ○

Views ○ ○ ○ ○ ○ ○ ○ ○ ○ ○

Difficulty of walk ○ ○ ○ ○ ○ ○ ○ ○ ○ ○

Highlights

Comments

Zoom in & out on the map using ➕ & ➖
Navigate map using ▲ ◀ ▼ ▶

EDGEBOROUGH

Height (m): 45m
OS Grid Reference: ST202285 · OS Grid Ref 10: ST2029428557
Flush bracket No: S3733

Date	Parking ★★★★★★	Map Ref: /47\

Start Time	Trig Time

Descent Start Time	Finish Time

Ascent Duration	Descent Duration	Total Time

Total Distance Covered	No. Of Steps

Companions

	Trig Condition ★★★★★★

Weather	Difficulty to find ★★★★★★

Enjoyment ◯ ◯ ◯ ◯ ◯ ◯ ◯ ◯ ◯ ◯

Views ◯ ◯ ◯ ◯ ◯ ◯ ◯ ◯ ◯ ◯

Difficulty of walk ◯ ◯ ◯ ◯ ◯ ◯ ◯ ◯ ◯ ◯

Highlights

Comments

Zoom in & out on the map using ➕ & ➖
Navigate map using ▲ ◀ ▼ ▶

ELSWORTHY

Height (m): 444m
OS Grid Reference: SS812415 · OS Grid Ref 10: SS8121941514
Flush bracket No: S5034

Date	Parking ★ ★ ★ ★ ★	Map Ref: △ 48

Start Time	Trig Time

Descent Start Time	Finish Time

Ascent Duration	Descent Duration	Total Time

Total Distance Covered	No. Of Steps

Companions

	Trig Condition ★ ★ ★ ★ ★

Weather	Difficulty to find ★ ★ ★ ★ ★

Enjoyment ○ ○ ○ ○ ○ ○ ○ ○ ○ ○

Views ○ ○ ○ ○ ○ ○ ○ ○ ○ ○

Difficulty of walk ○ ○ ○ ○ ○ ○ ○ ○ ○ ○

Highlights

Comments

Zoom in & out on the map using ➕ & ➖
Navigate map using ▲ ◀ ▼ ▶

FROME RESR

Height (m): 134m
OS Grid Reference: ST764480 · OS Grid Ref 10: ST7647448088
Flush bracket No: S2488

Date	Parking ★★★★★	Map Ref: △49
Start Time		Trig Time
Descent Start Time		Finish Time
Ascent Duration	Descent Duration	Total Time
Total Distance Covered		No. Of Steps
Companions		
		Trig Condition ★★★★★
Weather		Difficulty to find ★★★★★

Enjoyment ○○○○○○○○○○

Views ○○○○○○○○○○

Difficulty of walk ○○○○○○○○○○

Highlights

Comments

Zoom in & out on the map using ➕ & ➖
Navigate map using ▲ ◀ ▼ ▶

GREAT NURCOTT

Height (m): 332m
OS Grid Reference: SS909355 · OS Grid Ref 10: SS9096835584
Flush bracket No: S3913

Date	Parking ★ ★ ★ ★ ★	Map Ref: △50

Start Time	Trig Time

Descent Start Time	Finish Time

Ascent Duration	Descent Duration	Total Time

Total Distance Covered	No. Of Steps

Companions

	Trig Condition ★ ★ ★ ★ ★

Weather	Difficulty to find ★ ★ ★ ★ ★

Enjoyment ◯ ◯ ◯ ◯ ◯ ◯ ◯ ◯ ◯ ◯

Views ◯ ◯ ◯ ◯ ◯ ◯ ◯ ◯ ◯ ◯

Difficulty of walk ◯ ◯ ◯ ◯ ◯ ◯ ◯ ◯ ◯ ◯

Highlights

Comments

Zoom in & out on the map using ➕ & ➖
Navigate map using ▲ ◀ ▼ ▶

HADDON BEACON

Height (m): 355m
OS Grid Reference: SS961286 · OS Grid Ref 10: SS9614928605
Flush bracket No: S3916

Date	Parking ☆☆☆☆☆	Map Ref: /51\

Start Time	Trig Time

Descent Start Time	Finish Time

Ascent Duration	Descent Duration	Total Time

Total Distance Covered	No. Of Steps

Companions

	Trig Condition ☆☆☆☆☆

Weather	Difficulty to find ☆☆☆☆☆

Enjoyment ○ ○ ○ ○ ○ ○ ○ ○ ○ ○

Views ○ ○ ○ ○ ○ ○ ○ ○ ○ ○

Difficulty of walk ○ ○ ○ ○ ○ ○ ○ ○ ○ ○

Highlights

Comments

Zoom in & out on the map using ➕ & ➖
Navigate map using ▲ ◀ ▼ ▶

HERNE HILL

Height (m): 106m
OS Grid Reference: ST352138 • OS Grid Ref 10: ST3524813858
Flush bracket No: S3739

Date	Parking ★ ★ ★ ★ ★	Map Ref: /52\
Start Time	Trig Time	
Descent Start Time	Finish Time	
Ascent Duration	Descent Duration	Total Time
Total Distance Covered		No. Of Steps
Companions		
	Trig Condition ★ ★ ★ ★ ★	
Weather	Difficulty to find ★ ★ ★ ★ ★	

Enjoyment ○ ○ ○ ○ ○ ○ ○ ○ ○ ○

Views ○ ○ ○ ○ ○ ○ ○ ○ ○ ○

Difficulty of walk ○ ○ ○ ○ ○ ○ ○ ○ ○ ○

Highlights

Comments

Zoom in & out on the map using ➕ & ➖
Navigate map using ▲ ◄ ▼ ►

HIGHER WHITEFIELD FARM

Height (m): 310m
OS Grid Reference: ST065303 • OS Grid Ref 10: ST0654630307
Flush bracket No: S3729

Date	Parking ★★★★★	Map Ref: /53\

Start Time	Trig Time

Descent Start Time	Finish Time

Ascent Duration	Descent Duration	Total Time

Total Distance Covered	No. Of Steps

Companions

Trig Condition ★★★★★

Weather   Difficulty to find ★★★★★

Enjoyment ○○○○○○○○○○

Views ○○○○○○○○○○

Difficulty of walk ○○○○○○○○○○

Highlights

Comments

Zoom in & out on the map using ➕ & ➖
Navigate map using ▲ ◀ ▼ ▶

HOME FARM

Height (m): 69m
OS Grid Reference: ST706649 · OS Grid Ref 10: ST7060464932
Flush bracket No: S4023

Date	Parking ★ ★ ★ ★ ★	Map Ref: 54

Start Time	Trig Time

Descent Start Time	Finish Time

Ascent Duration	Descent Duration	Total Time

Total Distance Covered	No. Of Steps

Companions

	Trig Condition ★ ★ ★ ★ ★

Weather	Difficulty to find ★ ★ ★ ★ ★

Enjoyment ○ ○ ○ ○ ○ ○ ○ ○ ○ ○

Views ○ ○ ○ ○ ○ ○ ○ ○ ○ ○

Difficulty of walk ○ ○ ○ ○ ○ ○ ○ ○ ○ ○

Highlights

Comments

Zoom in & out on the map using ➕ & ➖
Navigate map using ▲ ◀ ▼ ▶

HONEYGAR

Height (m): 4m
OS Grid Reference: ST426427 · OS Grid Ref 10: ST4266842799
Flush bracket No: S3243

Date	Parking ★ ★ ★ ★ ★	Map Ref: /55\

Start Time	Trig Time

Descent Start Time	Finish Time

Ascent Duration	Descent Duration	Total Time

Total Distance Covered	No. Of Steps

Companions

	Trig Condition ★ ★ ★ ★ ★

Weather	Difficulty to find ★ ★ ★ ★ ★

Enjoyment ○ ○ ○ ○ ○ ○ ○ ○ ○

Views ○ ○ ○ ○ ○ ○ ○ ○ ○

Difficulty of walk ○ ○ ○ ○ ○ ○ ○ ○ ○

Highlights

Comments

Zoom in & out on the map using ➕ & ➖
Navigate map using ▲ ◀ ▼ ▶

55

HUNTSPILL

Height (m): 5m
OS Grid Reference: ST324453 • OS Grid Ref 10: ST3241545398
Flush bracket No:

Date	Parking ★ ★ ★ ★ ★	Map Ref: /56\

Start Time	Trig Time

Descent Start Time	Finish Time

Ascent Duration	Descent Duration	Total Time

Total Distance Covered	No. Of Steps

Companions

Trig Condition ★ ★ ★ ★ ★

Weather	Difficulty to find ★ ★ ★ ★ ★

Enjoyment ◯ ◯ ◯ ◯ ◯ ◯ ◯ ◯ ◯ ◯

Views ◯ ◯ ◯ ◯ ◯ ◯ ◯ ◯ ◯ ◯

Difficulty of walk ◯ ◯ ◯ ◯ ◯ ◯ ◯ ◯ ◯ ◯

Highlights

Comments

Zoom in & out on the map using ➕ & ➖
Navigate map using ▲ ◀ ▼ ▶

KELSTON ROUND HILL

Height (m): 218m
OS Grid Reference: ST710674 • OS Grid Ref 10: ST7102967481
Flush bracket No: S4022

Date	Parking ☆☆☆☆☆	Map Ref: △ 57

Start Time	Trig Time

Descent Start Time	Finish Time

Ascent Duration	Descent Duration	Total Time

Total Distance Covered	No. Of Steps

Companions

Trig Condition ☆☆☆☆☆

Weather	Difficulty to find ☆☆☆☆☆

Enjoyment ○○○○○○○○○○

Views ○○○○○○○○○○

Difficulty of walk ○○○○○○○○○○

Highlights

Comments

Zoom in & out on the map using ➕ & ➖
Navigate map using ▲ ◀ ▼ ▶

KINGS

Height (m): 49m
OS Grid Reference: ST169255 · OS Grid Ref 10: ST1691725532
Flush bracket No: S3915

Date	Parking ★ ★ ★ ★ ★	Map Ref: 58

Start Time	Trig Time

Descent Start Time	Finish Time

Ascent Duration	Descent Duration	Total Time

Total Distance Covered	No. Of Steps

Companions

	Trig Condition ★ ★ ★ ★ ★

Weather	Difficulty to find ★ ★ ★ ★ ★

Enjoyment ○ ○ ○ ○ ○ ○ ○ ○ ○ ○

Views ○ ○ ○ ○ ○ ○ ○ ○ ○ ○

Difficulty of walk ○ ○ ○ ○ ○ ○ ○ ○ ○ ○

Highlights

Comments

Zoom in & out on the map using ➕ & ➖
Navigate map using ▲ ◀ ▼ ▶

KINGSDON HILL

Height (m): 87m
OS Grid Reference: ST511266 · OS Grid Ref 10: ST5111126673
Flush bracket No: S5893

Date	Parking ★ ★ ★ ★ ★	Map Ref: /59\

Start Time	Trig Time

Descent Start Time	Finish Time

Ascent Duration	Descent Duration	Total Time

Total Distance Covered	No. Of Steps

Companions

Trig Condition ★ ★ ★ ★ ★

Weather	Difficulty to find ★ ★ ★ ★ ★

Enjoyment ◯ ◯ ◯ ◯ ◯ ◯ ◯ ◯ ◯ ◯

Views ◯ ◯ ◯ ◯ ◯ ◯ ◯ ◯ ◯ ◯

Difficulty of walk ◯ ◯ ◯ ◯ ◯ ◯ ◯ ◯ ◯ ◯

Highlights

Comments

Zoom in & out on the map using ➕ & ➖
Navigate map using ▲ ◀ ▼ ▶

LEIGH FARM

Height (m): 150m
OS Grid Reference: ST351061 · OS Grid Ref 10: ST3510406138
Flush bracket No: S3727

Date	Parking ★ ★ ★ ★ ★	Map Ref: /60\

Start Time	Trig Time

Descent Start Time	Finish Time

Ascent Duration	Descent Duration	Total Time

Total Distance Covered	No. Of Steps

Companions

	Trig Condition ★ ★ ★ ★ ★

Weather	Difficulty to find ★ ★ ★ ★ ★

Enjoyment ○ ○ ○ ○ ○ ○ ○ ○ ○ ○

Views ○ ○ ○ ○ ○ ○ ○ ○ ○ ○

Difficulty of walk ○ ○ ○ ○ ○ ○ ○ ○ ○ ○

Highlights

Comments

Zoom in & out on the map using ➕ & ➖
Navigate map using ▲ ◀ ▼ ▶

LOLLOVER HILL

Height (m): 90m
OS Grid Reference: ST474324 · OS Grid Ref 10: ST4740332476
Flush bracket No: S5891

Date	Parking ★★★★★	Map Ref: 61

Start Time	Trig Time

Descent Start Time	Finish Time

Ascent Duration	Descent Duration	Total Time

Total Distance Covered	No. Of Steps

Companions

	Trig Condition ★★★★★

Weather	Difficulty to find ★★★★★

Enjoyment ○○○○○○○○○○

Views ○○○○○○○○○○

Difficulty of walk ○○○○○○○○○○

Highlights

Comments

Zoom in & out on the map using ➕ & ➖
Navigate map using ▲ ◀ ▼ ▶

LOXTON HILL

Height (m): 175m
OS Grid Reference: ST365570 • OS Grid Ref 10: ST3656057052
Flush bracket No: S3248

Date	Parking ★ ★ ★ ★ ★	Map Ref: △62

Start Time	Trig Time

Descent Start Time	Finish Time

Ascent Duration	Descent Duration	Total Time

Total Distance Covered	No. Of Steps

Companions

	Trig Condition ★ ★ ★ ★ ★

Weather	Difficulty to find ★ ★ ★ ★ ★

Enjoyment ◯ ◯ ◯ ◯ ◯ ◯ ◯ ◯ ◯ ◯

Views ◯ ◯ ◯ ◯ ◯ ◯ ◯ ◯ ◯ ◯

Difficulty of walk ◯ ◯ ◯ ◯ ◯ ◯ ◯ ◯ ◯ ◯

Highlights

Comments

Zoom in & out on the map using ➕ & ➖
Navigate map using ▲ ◀ ▼ ▶

LYPE HILL

Height (m): 424m
OS Grid Reference: SS950371 · OS Grid Ref 10: SS9503537111
Flush bracket No: S3930

Date	Parking ★ ★ ★ ★ ★	Map Ref: 63

Start Time	Trig Time

Descent Start Time	Finish Time

Ascent Duration	Descent Duration	Total Time

Total Distance Covered	No. Of Steps

Companions

	Trig Condition ★ ★ ★ ★ ★

Weather	Difficulty to find ★ ★ ★ ★ ★

Enjoyment ○ ○ ○ ○ ○ ○ ○ ○ ○ ○

Views ○ ○ ○ ○ ○ ○ ○ ○ ○ ○

Difficulty of walk ○ ○ ○ ○ ○ ○ ○ ○ ○ ○

Highlights

Comments

Zoom in & out on the map using ➕ & ➖
Navigate map using ▲ ◀ ▼ ▶

MAES KNOLL

Height (m): 198m
OS Grid Reference: ST600660 · OS Grid Ref 10: ST6009566083
Flush bracket No: S9526

Date	Parking ★★★★★	Map Ref: /64\

Start Time	Trig Time

Descent Start Time	Finish Time

Ascent Duration	Descent Duration	Total Time

Total Distance Covered	No. Of Steps

Companions

	Trig Condition ★★★★★

Weather	Difficulty to find ★★★★★

Enjoyment ○○○○○○○○○○

Views ○○○○○○○○○○

Difficulty of walk ○○○○○○○○○○

Highlights

Comments

Zoom in & out on the map using ➕ & ➖
Navigate map using ▲ ◀ ▼ ▶

MENDIP GOLF LINKS

Height (m): 297m
OS Grid Reference: ST619467 · OS Grid Ref 10: ST6194046752
Flush bracket No: S2547

Date	Parking ⭐⭐⭐⭐⭐	Map Ref: /65\

Start Time	Trig Time

Descent Start Time	Finish Time

Ascent Duration	Descent Duration	Total Time

Total Distance Covered	No. Of Steps

Companions

	Trig Condition ⭐⭐⭐⭐⭐

Weather	Difficulty to find ⭐⭐⭐⭐⭐

Enjoyment ◯◯◯◯◯◯◯◯◯◯

Views ◯◯◯◯◯◯◯◯◯◯

Difficulty of walk ◯◯◯◯◯◯◯◯◯◯

Highlights

Comments

Zoom in & out on the map using ➕ & ➖
Navigate map using ▲ ◀ ▼ ▶

MERRIDGE

Height (m): 211m
OS Grid Reference: ST209354 • OS Grid Ref 10: ST2092435414
Flush bracket No: S3245

Date	Parking ★ ★ ★ ★ ★	Map Ref: /66\

Start Time	Trig Time

Descent Start Time	Finish Time

Ascent Duration	Descent Duration	Total Time

Total Distance Covered	No. Of Steps

Companions

	Trig Condition ★ ★ ★ ★ ★

Weather	Difficulty to find ★ ★ ★ ★ ★

Enjoyment ○ ○ ○ ○ ○ ○ ○ ○ ○ ○

Views ○ ○ ○ ○ ○ ○ ○ ○ ○ ○

Difficulty of walk ○ ○ ○ ○ ○ ○ ○ ○ ○ ○

Highlights

Comments

Zoom in & out on the map using ➕ & ➖
Navigate map using ▲ ◀ ▼ ▶

MIDDLE HOPE

Height (m): 48m
OS Grid Reference: ST327660 · OS Grid Ref 10: ST3270866046
Flush bracket No: S3269

Date	Parking ★★★★★	Map Ref: /67\

Start Time	Trig Time

Descent Start Time	Finish Time

Ascent Duration	Descent Duration	Total Time

Total Distance Covered	No. Of Steps

Companions

	Trig Condition ★★★★★

Weather	Difficulty to find ★★★★★

Enjoyment ○ ○ ○ ○ ○ ○ ○ ○ ○ ○

Views ○ ○ ○ ○ ○ ○ ○ ○ ○ ○

Difficulty of walk ○ ○ ○ ○ ○ ○ ○ ○ ○ ○

Highlights

Comments

Zoom in & out on the map using ➕ & ➖
Navigate map using ▲ ◀ ▼ ▶

NEW PLANTATION

Height (m): 78m
OS Grid Reference: ST490100 · OS Grid Ref 10: ST4900910029
Flush bracket No: S5525

Date	Parking ★ ★ ★ ★ ★	Map Ref: /68\

Start Time	Trig Time

Descent Start Time	Finish Time

Ascent Duration	Descent Duration	Total Time

Total Distance Covered	No. Of Steps

Companions

	Trig Condition ★ ★ ★ ★ ★

Weather	Difficulty to find ★ ★ ★ ★ ★

Enjoyment ○ ○ ○ ○ ○ ○ ○ ○ ○ ○

Views ○ ○ ○ ○ ○ ○ ○ ○ ○ ○

Difficulty of walk ○ ○ ○ ○ ○ ○ ○ ○ ○ ○

Highlights

Comments

Zoom in & out on the map using ➕ & ➖
Navigate map using ▲ ◀ ▼ ▶

NORTH HILL

Height (m): 165m
OS Grid Reference: ST573670 • OS Grid Ref 10: ST5732867040
Flush bracket No: S3372

Date	Parking ☆☆☆☆☆	Map Ref: /69\

Start Time	Trig Time

Descent Start Time	Finish Time

Ascent Duration	Descent Duration	Total Time

Total Distance Covered	No. Of Steps

Companions

	Trig Condition ☆☆☆☆☆

Weather	Difficulty to find ☆☆☆☆☆

Enjoyment ○○○○○○○○○○

Views ○○○○○○○○○○

Difficulty of walk ○○○○○○○○○○

Highlights

Comments

Zoom in & out on the map using ➕ & ➖
Navigate map using ▲ ◀ ▼ ▶

NYLAND HILL

Height (m): 77m
OS Grid Reference: ST457503 · OS Grid Ref 10: ST4578150394
Flush bracket No: S3257

Date	Parking ★ ★ ★ ★ ★	Map Ref: 70

Start Time	Trig Time

Descent Start Time	Finish Time

Ascent Duration	Descent Duration	Total Time

Total Distance Covered	No. Of Steps

Companions

	Trig Condition ★ ★ ★ ★ ★

Weather	Difficulty to find ★ ★ ★ ★ ★

Enjoyment ○ ○ ○ ○ ○ ○ ○ ○ ○ ○

Views ○ ○ ○ ○ ○ ○ ○ ○ ○ ○

Difficulty of walk ○ ○ ○ ○ ○ ○ ○ ○ ○ ○

Highlights

Comments

Zoom in & out on the map using ➕ & ➖
Navigate map using ▲ ◀ ▼ ▶

PAULTON

Height (m): 156m
OS Grid Reference: ST645558 • OS Grid Ref 10: ST6459855848
Flush bracket No: S2402

Date	Parking ☆☆☆☆☆	Map Ref: /71\

Start Time	Trig Time

Descent Start Time	Finish Time

Ascent Duration	Descent Duration	Total Time

Total Distance Covered	No. Of Steps

Companions

	Trig Condition ☆☆☆☆☆

Weather	Difficulty to find ☆☆☆☆☆

Enjoyment ○ ○ ○ ○ ○ ○ ○ ○ ○ ○

Views ○ ○ ○ ○ ○ ○ ○ ○ ○ ○

Difficulty of walk ○ ○ ○ ○ ○ ○ ○ ○ ○ ○

Highlights

Comments

Zoom in & out on the map using ➕ & ➖
Navigate map using ▲ ◀ ▼ ▶

PAWLETT

Height (m): 33m
OS Grid Reference: ST291430 • OS Grid Ref 10: ST2912443068
Flush bracket No: S3259

Date	Parking ★ ★ ★ ★ ★	Map Ref: /72\

Start Time	Trig Time

Descent Start Time	Finish Time

Ascent Duration	Descent Duration	Total Time

Total Distance Covered	No. Of Steps

Companions

Trig Condition ★ ★ ★ ★ ★

Weather	Difficulty to find ★ ★ ★ ★ ★

Enjoyment ○ ○ ○ ○ ○ ○ ○ ○ ○ ○

Views ○ ○ ○ ○ ○ ○ ○ ○ ○ ○

Difficulty of walk ○ ○ ○ ○ ○ ○ ○ ○ ○ ○

Highlights

Comments

Zoom in & out on the map using ➕ & ➖
Navigate map using ▲ ◀ ▼ ▶

PEN HILL

Height (m): 306m
OS Grid Reference: ST564487 · OS Grid Ref 10: ST5644348779
Flush bracket No: S1515

Date	Parking ⭐⭐⭐⭐⭐	Map Ref: △ 73

Start Time | Trig Time

Descent Start Time | Finish Time

Ascent Duration | Descent Duration | Total Time

Total Distance Covered | No. Of Steps

Companions

Trig Condition ⭐⭐⭐⭐⭐

Weather | Difficulty to find ⭐⭐⭐⭐⭐

Enjoyment ○○○○○○○○○○

Views ○○○○○○○○○○

Difficulty of walk ○○○○○○○○○○

Highlights

Comments

Zoom in & out on the map using ➕ & ➖
Navigate map using ▲ ◀ ▼ ▶

PENNARD HILL

Height (m): 143m
OS Grid Reference: ST613372 · OS Grid Ref 10: ST6130737220
Flush bracket No: S5915

Date	Parking ★ ★ ★ ★ ★	Map Ref: /74\

Start Time	Trig Time

Descent Start Time	Finish Time

Ascent Duration	Descent Duration	Total Time

Total Distance Covered	No. Of Steps

Companions

	Trig Condition ★ ★ ★ ★ ★

Weather	Difficulty to find ★ ★ ★ ★ ★

Enjoyment ○ ○ ○ ○ ○ ○ ○ ○ ○ ○

Views ○ ○ ○ ○ ○ ○ ○ ○ ○ ○

Difficulty of walk ○ ○ ○ ○ ○ ○ ○ ○ ○ ○

Highlights

Comments

Zoom in & out on the map using ⊞ & ⊟
Navigate map using ▲ ◄ ▼ ►

PENSELWOOD

Height (m): 201m
OS Grid Reference: ST757305 · OS Grid Ref 10: ST7573030501
Flush bracket No: S5878

Date	Parking	Map Ref: 75

Start Time		Trig Time

Descent Start Time		Finish Time

Ascent Duration	Descent Duration	Total Time

Total Distance Covered		No. Of Steps

Companions

	Trig Condition
Weather	Difficulty to find

Enjoyment	○ ○ ○ ○ ○ ○ ○ ○ ○ ○
Views	○ ○ ○ ○ ○ ○ ○ ○ ○ ○
Difficulty of walk	○ ○ ○ ○ ○ ○ ○ ○ ○ ○

Highlights

Comments

Zoom in & out on the map using ➕ & ➖
Navigate map using ▲ ◀ ▼ ▶

PERRITON HILL

Height (m): 296m
OS Grid Reference: SS948442 · OS Grid Ref 10: SS9482444225
Flush bracket No: S3758

Date	Parking ★ ★ ★ ★ ★	Map Ref: /76

Start Time	Trig Time

Descent Start Time	Finish Time

Ascent Duration	Descent Duration	Total Time

Total Distance Covered	No. Of Steps

Companions

	Trig Condition ★ ★ ★ ★ ★

Weather	Difficulty to find ★ ★ ★ ★ ★

Enjoyment ◯ ◯ ◯ ◯ ◯ ◯ ◯ ◯ ◯ ◯

Views ◯ ◯ ◯ ◯ ◯ ◯ ◯ ◯ ◯ ◯

Difficulty of walk ◯ ◯ ◯ ◯ ◯ ◯ ◯ ◯ ◯ ◯

Highlights

Comments

Zoom in & out on the map using ➕ & ➖
Navigate map using ▲ ◀ ▼ ▶

PILTON

Height (m): 121m
OS Grid Reference: ST593414 • OS Grid Ref 10: ST5932541439
Flush bracket No: S5914

Date	Parking	Map Ref: /77\

Start Time	Trig Time

Descent Start Time	Finish Time

Ascent Duration	Descent Duration	Total Time

Total Distance Covered	No. Of Steps

Companions

Trig Condition

Weather | Difficulty to find

Enjoyment ○○○○○○○○○○

Views ○○○○○○○○○○

Difficulty of walk ○○○○○○○○○○

Highlights

Comments

Zoom in & out on the map using ➕ & ➖
Navigate map using ▲ ◀ ▼ ▶

PINNACLE HILL

Height (m): 96m
OS Grid Reference: ST201403 • OS Grid Ref 10: ST2012540374
Flush bracket No: S3255

Date	Parking ★ ★ ★ ★ ★	Map Ref: /78\

Start Time	Trig Time

Descent Start Time	Finish Time

Ascent Duration	Descent Duration	Total Time

Total Distance Covered	No. Of Steps

Companions

	Trig Condition ★ ★ ★ ★ ★

Weather	Difficulty to find ★ ★ ★ ★ ★

Enjoyment ○ ○ ○ ○ ○ ○ ○ ○ ○

Views ○ ○ ○ ○ ○ ○ ○ ○ ○

Difficulty of walk ○ ○ ○ ○ ○ ○ ○ ○ ○

Highlights

Comments

Zoom in & out on the map using ➕ & ➖
Navigate map using ▲ ◀ ▼ ▶

PLANTATION FARM

Height (m): 73m
OS Grid Reference: ST462287 • OS Grid Ref 10: ST4625828774
Flush bracket No: S5895

Date	Parking ⭐⭐⭐⭐⭐	Map Ref: △79

Start Time	Trig Time

Descent Start Time	Finish Time

Ascent Duration	Descent Duration	Total Time

Total Distance Covered	No. Of Steps

Companions

	Trig Condition ⭐⭐⭐⭐⭐
Weather	Difficulty to find ⭐⭐⭐⭐⭐

Enjoyment ○ ○ ○ ○ ○ ○ ○ ○ ○ ○

Views ○ ○ ○ ○ ○ ○ ○ ○ ○ ○

Difficulty of walk ○ ○ ○ ○ ○ ○ ○ ○ ○ ○

Highlights

Comments

Zoom in & out on the map using ➕ & ➖
Navigate map using ▲ ◀ ▼ ▶

POSTLEBURY

Height (m): 197m
OS Grid Reference: ST735429 · OS Grid Ref 10: ST7357742938
Flush bracket No: S3219

Date	Parking ★ ★ ★ ★ ★	Map Ref: /80\

Start Time	Trig Time

Descent Start Time	Finish Time

Ascent Duration	Descent Duration	Total Time

Total Distance Covered	No. Of Steps

Companions

	Trig Condition ★ ★ ★ ★ ★

Weather	Difficulty to find ★ ★ ★ ★ ★

Enjoyment ○ ○ ○ ○ ○ ○ ○ ○ ○ ○

Views ○ ○ ○ ○ ○ ○ ○ ○ ○ ○

Difficulty of walk ○ ○ ○ ○ ○ ○ ○ ○ ○ ○

Highlights

Comments

Zoom in & out on the map using ➕ & ➖
Navigate map using ▲ ◀ ▼ ▶

POTTERSHILL

Height (m): 203m
OS Grid Reference: ST505665 · OS Grid Ref 10: ST5057766503
Flush bracket No: S3272

Date	Parking ★★★★★	Map Ref: /81\

Start Time	Trig Time

Descent Start Time	Finish Time

Ascent Duration	Descent Duration	Total Time

Total Distance Covered	No. Of Steps

Companions

	Trig Condition ★★★★★

Weather	Difficulty to find ★★★★★

Enjoyment ○ ○ ○ ○ ○ ○ ○ ○ ○ ○

Views ○ ○ ○ ○ ○ ○ ○ ○ ○ ○

Difficulty of walk ○ ○ ○ ○ ○ ○ ○ ○ ○ ○

Highlights

Comments

Zoom in & out on the map using ➕ & ➖
Navigate map using ▲ ◀ ▼ ▶

PYNCOMBE FARM

Height (m): 281m
OS Grid Reference: ST064257 · OS Grid Ref 10: ST0642725734
Flush bracket No: S3736

Date	Parking ★ ★ ★ ★ ★	Map Ref: /82\

Start Time	Trig Time

Descent Start Time	Finish Time

Ascent Duration	Descent Duration	Total Time

Total Distance Covered	No. Of Steps

Companions	

	Trig Condition ★ ★ ★ ★ ★

Weather	Difficulty to find ★ ★ ★ ★ ★

Enjoyment ◯ ◯ ◯ ◯ ◯ ◯ ◯ ◯ ◯ ◯

Views ◯ ◯ ◯ ◯ ◯ ◯ ◯ ◯ ◯ ◯

Difficulty of walk ◯ ◯ ◯ ◯ ◯ ◯ ◯ ◯ ◯ ◯

Highlights

Comments

Zoom in & out on the map using ➕ & ➖
Navigate map using ▲ ◀ ▼ ▶

RAINBOW WOOD

Height (m): 167m
OS Grid Reference: ST766637 • OS Grid Ref 10: ST7664363729
Flush bracket No: S4021

Date	Parking ★★★★★★	Map Ref: /83\

Start Time	Trig Time

Descent Start Time	Finish Time

Ascent Duration	Descent Duration	Total Time

Total Distance Covered	No. Of Steps

Companions

	Trig Condition ★★★★★★

Weather	Difficulty to find ★★★★★★

Enjoyment	○○○○○○○○○○
Views	○○○○○○○○○○
Difficulty of walk	○○○○○○○○○○

Highlights

Comments

Zoom in & out on the map using ➕ & ➖
Navigate map using ▲ ◀ ▼ ▶

REDLYNCH

Height (m): 161m
OS Grid Reference: ST697335 · OS Grid Ref 10: ST6978033570
Flush bracket No: S5911

Date	Parking ★ ★ ★ ★ ★	Map Ref: /84\

Start Time	Trig Time

Descent Start Time	Finish Time

Ascent Duration	Descent Duration	Total Time

Total Distance Covered	No. Of Steps

Companions

	Trig Condition ★ ★ ★ ★ ★

Weather	Difficulty to find ★ ★ ★ ★ ★

Enjoyment ○ ○ ○ ○ ○ ○ ○ ○ ○ ○

Views ○ ○ ○ ○ ○ ○ ○ ○ ○ ○

Difficulty of walk ○ ○ ○ ○ ○ ○ ○ ○ ○ ○

Highlights

Comments

Zoom in & out on the map using ➕ & ➖
Navigate map using ▲ ◀ ▼ ▶

ROCK

Height (m): 86m
OS Grid Reference: ST329229 • OS Grid Ref 10: ST3292822910
Flush bracket No: S3732

Date	Parking ⭐⭐⭐⭐⭐	Map Ref: /85\

Start Time	Trig Time

Descent Start Time	Finish Time

Ascent Duration	Descent Duration	Total Time

Total Distance Covered	No. Of Steps

Companions

	Trig Condition ⭐⭐⭐⭐⭐

Weather	Difficulty to find ⭐⭐⭐⭐⭐

Enjoyment ◯◯◯◯◯◯◯◯◯◯

Views ◯◯◯◯◯◯◯◯◯◯

Difficulty of walk ◯◯◯◯◯◯◯◯◯◯

Highlights

Comments

Zoom in & out on the map using ➕ & ➖
Navigate map using ▲ ◀ ▼ ▶

RYDON HILL

Height (m): 87m
OS Grid Reference: ST092425 • OS Grid Ref 10: ST0925442539
Flush bracket No: S3747

Date	Parking ★ ★ ★ ★ ★	Map Ref: △ 86
Start Time	Trig Time	
Descent Start Time	Finish Time	
Ascent Duration	Descent Duration	Total Time
Total Distance Covered	No. Of Steps	
Companions		
	Trig Condition ★ ★ ★ ★ ★	
Weather	Difficulty to find ★ ★ ★ ★ ★	

Enjoyment ◯ ◯ ◯ ◯ ◯ ◯ ◯ ◯ ◯ ◯

Views ◯ ◯ ◯ ◯ ◯ ◯ ◯ ◯ ◯ ◯

Difficulty of walk ◯ ◯ ◯ ◯ ◯ ◯ ◯ ◯ ◯ ◯

Highlights

Comments

Zoom in & out on the map using ➕ & ➖
Navigate map using ▲ ◀ ▼ ▶

SELWORTHY BEACON

Height (m): 309m
OS Grid Reference: SS918479 · OS Grid Ref 10: SS9188647988
Flush bracket No: S3944

Date	Parking ★ ★ ★ ★ ★ ★	Map Ref: /87\

Start Time	Trig Time

Descent Start Time	Finish Time

Ascent Duration	Descent Duration	Total Time

Total Distance Covered	No. Of Steps

Companions

	Trig Condition ★ ★ ★ ★ ★

Weather	Difficulty to find ★ ★ ★ ★ ★

Enjoyment ◯ ◯ ◯ ◯ ◯ ◯ ◯ ◯ ◯ ◯

Views ◯ ◯ ◯ ◯ ◯ ◯ ◯ ◯ ◯ ◯

Difficulty of walk ◯ ◯ ◯ ◯ ◯ ◯ ◯ ◯ ◯ ◯

Highlights

Comments

Zoom in & out on the map using ➕ & ➖
Navigate map using ▲ ◀ ▼ ▶

SHAPWICK

Height (m): 98m
OS Grid Reference: ST386381 · OS Grid Ref 10: ST3867338155
Flush bracket No: S3231

Date	Parking ★★★★★	Map Ref: /88\

Start Time	Trig Time

Descent Start Time	Finish Time

Ascent Duration	Descent Duration	Total Time

Total Distance Covered	No. Of Steps

Companions	

	Trig Condition ★★★★★

Weather	Difficulty to find ★★★★★

Enjoyment ○○○○○○○○○○

Views ○○○○○○○○○○

Difficulty of walk ○○○○○○○○○○

Highlights

Comments

Zoom in & out on the map using ➕ & ➖
Navigate map using ▲ ◀ ▼ ▶

SMALL DOWN KNOLL

Height (m): 222m
OS Grid Reference: ST665406 · OS Grid Ref 10: ST6651840609
Flush bracket No: S5834

Date	Parking ★★★★★	Map Ref: /89\

Start Time	Trig Time

Descent Start Time	Finish Time

Ascent Duration	Descent Duration	Total Time

Total Distance Covered	No. Of Steps

Companions

	Trig Condition ★★★★★

Weather	Difficulty to find ★★★★★

Enjoyment ○○○○○○○○○○

Views ○○○○○○○○○○

Difficulty of walk ○○○○○○○○○○

Highlights

Comments

Zoom in & out on the map using ⊞ & ⊟
Navigate map using ▲ ◀ ▼ ▶

SNOWDON HILL

Height (m): 219m
OS Grid Reference: ST308091 · OS Grid Ref 10: ST3083909124
Flush bracket No: S3726

Date	Parking ★ ★ ★ ★ ★	Map Ref: /90\
Start Time	Trig Time	
Descent Start Time	Finish Time	
Ascent Duration	Descent Duration	Total Time
Total Distance Covered	No. Of Steps	
Companions		
	Trig Condition ★ ★ ★ ★ ★	
Weather	Difficulty to find ★ ★ ★ ★ ★	

Enjoyment ◯ ◯ ◯ ◯ ◯ ◯ ◯ ◯ ◯ ◯

Views ◯ ◯ ◯ ◯ ◯ ◯ ◯ ◯ ◯ ◯

Difficulty of walk ◯ ◯ ◯ ◯ ◯ ◯ ◯ ◯ ◯ ◯

Highlights

Comments

Zoom in & out on the map using ➕ & ➖
Navigate map using ▲ ◀ ▼ ▶

SOLSBURY HILL

Height (m): 188m
OS Grid Reference: ST767677 · OS Grid Ref 10: ST7678467788
Flush bracket No: S4066

Date	Parking ★★★★★	Map Ref: /91\

Start Time	Trig Time

Descent Start Time	Finish Time

Ascent Duration	Descent Duration	Total Time

Total Distance Covered	No. Of Steps

Companions

	Trig Condition ★★★★★

Weather	Difficulty to find ★★★★★

Enjoyment ○○○○○○○○○○

Views ○○○○○○○○○○

Difficulty of walk ○○○○○○○○○○

Highlights

Comments

Zoom in & out on the map using ➕ & ➖
Navigate map using ▲ ◀ ▼ ▶

ST RAYN HILL

Height (m): 238m
OS Grid Reference: ST399098 • OS Grid Ref 10: ST3995909812
Flush bracket No: S3946

Date	Parking ★ ★ ★ ★ ★	Map Ref: /92\

Start Time	Trig Time

Descent Start Time	Finish Time

Ascent Duration	Descent Duration	Total Time

Total Distance Covered	No. Of Steps

Companions	

	Trig Condition ★ ★ ★ ★ ★

Weather	Difficulty to find ★ ★ ★ ★ ★

Enjoyment ○ ○ ○ ○ ○ ○ ○ ○ ○ ○

Views ○ ○ ○ ○ ○ ○ ○ ○ ○ ○

Difficulty of walk ○ ○ ○ ○ ○ ○ ○ ○ ○ ○

Highlights

Comments

Zoom in & out on the map using 🞢 & 🞨
Navigate map using ▲ ◀ ▼ ▶

STAPLE HILL

Height (m): 316m
OS Grid Reference: ST240166 • OS Grid Ref 10: ST2404116681
Flush bracket No: S3970

Date	Parking ★★★★★	Map Ref: 93

Start Time	Trig Time

Descent Start Time	Finish Time

Ascent Duration	Descent Duration	Total Time

Total Distance Covered	No. Of Steps

Companions

	Trig Condition ★★★★★

Weather	Difficulty to find ★★★★★

Enjoyment ○○○○○○○○○○

Views ○○○○○○○○○○

Difficulty of walk ○○○○○○○○○○

Highlights

Comments

STEEP HOLME

Height (m): 78m
OS Grid Reference: ST229607 • OS Grid Ref 10: ST2290460717
Flush bracket No: S2484

Date	Parking ★ ★ ★ ★ ★	Map Ref: /94\

Start Time	Trig Time

Descent Start Time	Finish Time

Ascent Duration	Descent Duration	Total Time

Total Distance Covered	No. Of Steps

Companions

Trig Condition ★ ★ ★ ★ ★

Weather	Difficulty to find ★ ★ ★ ★ ★

Enjoyment ○ ○ ○ ○ ○ ○ ○ ○ ○ ○

Views ○ ○ ○ ○ ○ ○ ○ ○ ○ ○

Difficulty of walk ○ ○ ○ ○ ○ ○ ○ ○ ○ ○

Highlights

Comments

Zoom in & out on the map using ➕ & ➖
Navigate map using ▲ ◀ ▼ ▶

STOCKLINCH

Height (m): 96m
OS Grid Reference: ST392172 · OS Grid Ref 10: ST3923717294
Flush bracket No: S5052

Date	Parking ★★★★★	Map Ref: /95\

Start Time	Trig Time

Descent Start Time	Finish Time

Ascent Duration	Descent Duration	Total Time

Total Distance Covered	No. Of Steps

Companions

	Trig Condition ★★★★★

Weather	Difficulty to find ★★★★★

Enjoyment ○○○○○○○○○○

Views ○○○○○○○○○○

Difficulty of walk ○○○○○○○○○○

Highlights

Comments

Zoom in & out on the map using ➕ & ➖
Navigate map using ▲ ◀ ▼ ▶

STOKE HILL

Height (m): 96m
OS Grid Reference: ST269221 • OS Grid Ref 10: ST2693922161
Flush bracket No: S3969

Date	Parking ★ ★ ★ ★ ★	Map Ref: △96

Start Time	Trig Time

Descent Start Time	Finish Time

Ascent Duration	Descent Duration	Total Time

Total Distance Covered	No. Of Steps

Companions

Trig Condition ★ ★ ★ ★ ★

Weather | Difficulty to find ★ ★ ★ ★ ★

Enjoyment ○ ○ ○ ○ ○ ○ ○ ○ ○ ○

Views ○ ○ ○ ○ ○ ○ ○ ○ ○ ○

Difficulty of walk ○ ○ ○ ○ ○ ○ ○ ○ ○ ○

Highlights

Comments

Zoom in & out on the map using ▣ & ▣
Navigate map using ▲ ◀ ▼ ▶

STORRIDGE HILL

Height (m): 167m
OS Grid Reference: ST318046 · OS Grid Ref 10: ST3185104624
Flush bracket No: S3718

Date	Parking	Map Ref: /97\

Start Time		Trig Time

Descent Start Time		Finish Time

Ascent Duration	Descent Duration	Total Time

Total Distance Covered		No. Of Steps

Companions

	Trig Condition

Weather	Difficulty to find

Enjoyment ○ ○ ○ ○ ○ ○ ○ ○ ○

Views ○ ○ ○ ○ ○ ○ ○ ○ ○

Difficulty of walk ○ ○ ○ ○ ○ ○ ○ ○ ○

Highlights

Comments

Zoom in & out on the map using ➕ & ➖
Navigate map using ▲ ◀ ▼ ▶

TREBOROUGH COMMON

Height (m): 412m
OS Grid Reference: ST004351 • OS Grid Ref 10: ST0048635111
Flush bracket No: S3748

Date	Parking ★ ★ ★ ★ ★	Map Ref: /98\

Start Time	Trig Time

Descent Start Time	Finish Time

Ascent Duration	Descent Duration	Total Time

Total Distance Covered	No. Of Steps

Companions

	Trig Condition ★ ★ ★ ★ ★

Weather	Difficulty to find ★ ★ ★ ★ ★

Enjoyment ○ ○ ○ ○ ○ ○ ○ ○ ○ ○

Views ○ ○ ○ ○ ○ ○ ○ ○ ○ ○

Difficulty of walk ○ ○ ○ ○ ○ ○ ○ ○ ○ ○

Highlights

Comments

Zoom in & out on the map using ➕ & ➖
Navigate map using ▲ ◀ ▼ ▶

TWERTON HILL

Height (m): 141m
OS Grid Reference: ST724633 · OS Grid Ref 10: ST7249163326
Flush bracket No: S3230

Date	Parking ★★★★★	Map Ref: 99

Start Time	Trig Time

Descent Start Time	Finish Time

Ascent Duration	Descent Duration	Total Time

Total Distance Covered	No. Of Steps

Companions

	Trig Condition ★★★★★

Weather	Difficulty to find ★★★★★

Enjoyment ○○○○○○○○○○

Views ○○○○○○○○○○

Difficulty of walk ○○○○○○○○○○

Highlights

Comments

Zoom in & out on the map using ➕ & ➖
Navigate map using ▲ ◀ ▼ ▶

UNITY FARM

Height (m): 17m
OS Grid Reference: ST294541 • OS Grid Ref 10: ST2943154101
Flush bracket No: S3249

Date	Parking ★ ★ ★ ★ ★	Map Ref: △100

Start Time	Trig Time

Descent Start Time	Finish Time

Ascent Duration	Descent Duration	Total Time

Total Distance Covered	No. Of Steps

Companions

	Trig Condition ★ ★ ★ ★ ★

Weather	Difficulty to find ★ ★ ★ ★ ★

Enjoyment ○ ○ ○ ○ ○ ○ ○ ○ ○ ○

Views ○ ○ ○ ○ ○ ○ ○ ○ ○ ○

Difficulty of walk ○ ○ ○ ○ ○ ○ ○ ○ ○ ○

Highlights

Comments

Zoom in & out on the map using ⊞ & ⊟
Navigate map using ▲ ◄ ▼ ►

WALL COMMON

Height (m): 7m
OS Grid Reference: ST260453 • OS Grid Ref 10: ST2604745306
Flush bracket No: S3232

Date	Parking ★★★★★	Map Ref: △ 101

Start Time	Trig Time

Descent Start Time	Finish Time

Ascent Duration	Descent Duration	Total Time

Total Distance Covered	No. Of Steps

Companions

	Trig Condition ★★★★★

Weather	Difficulty to find ★★★★★

Enjoyment ○○○○○○○○○○

Views ○○○○○○○○○○

Difficulty of walk ○○○○○○○○○○

Highlights

Comments

Zoom in & out on the map using ➕ & ➖
Navigate map using ▲ ◀ ▼ ▶

WARREN FARM

Height (m): 84m
OS Grid Reference: ST045433 · OS Grid Ref 10: ST0456443373
Flush bracket No: S3756

Date	Parking ★ ★ ★ ★ ★	Map Ref: 102

Start Time	Trig Time

Descent Start Time	Finish Time

Ascent Duration	Descent Duration	Total Time

Total Distance Covered	No. Of Steps

Companions

	Trig Condition ★ ★ ★ ★ ★

Weather	Difficulty to find ★ ★ ★ ★ ★

Enjoyment ○ ○ ○ ○ ○ ○ ○ ○ ○ ○

Views ○ ○ ○ ○ ○ ○ ○ ○ ○ ○

Difficulty of walk ○ ○ ○ ○ ○ ○ ○ ○ ○ ○

Highlights

Comments

Zoom in & out on the map using ➕ & ➖
Navigate map using ▲ ◀ ▼ ▶

WAVERING DOWN

Height (m): 211m
OS Grid Reference: ST406559 • OS Grid Ref 10: ST4069955900
Flush bracket No: S3247

Date	Parking ★★★★★	Map Ref: △103

Start Time		Trig Time

Descent Start Time		Finish Time

Ascent Duration	Descent Duration	Total Time

Total Distance Covered		No. Of Steps

Companions

	Trig Condition ★★★★★

Weather	Difficulty to find ★★★★★

Enjoyment ○○○○○○○○○○

Views ○○○○○○○○○○

Difficulty of walk ○○○○○○○○○○

Highlights

Comments

Zoom in & out on the map using ➕ & ➖
Navigate map using ▲ ◀ ▼ ▶

WESTBURY BEACON

Height (m): 269m
OS Grid Reference: ST499507 · OS Grid Ref 10: ST4999950778
Flush bracket No: S3250

Date	Parking ★ ★ ★ ★ ★	Map Ref: △104

Start Time	Trig Time

Descent Start Time	Finish Time

Ascent Duration	Descent Duration	Total Time

Total Distance Covered	No. Of Steps

Companions	

	Trig Condition ★ ★ ★ ★ ★

Weather	Difficulty to find ★ ★ ★ ★ ★

Enjoyment ◯ ◯ ◯ ◯ ◯ ◯ ◯ ◯ ◯ ◯

Views ◯ ◯ ◯ ◯ ◯ ◯ ◯ ◯ ◯ ◯

Difficulty of walk ◯ ◯ ◯ ◯ ◯ ◯ ◯ ◯ ◯ ◯

Highlights

Comments

Zoom in & out on the map using ➕ & ➖
Navigate map using ▲ ◀ ▼ ▶

WESTON

Height (m): 122m
OS Grid Reference: ST721663 · OS Grid Ref 10: ST7219666312
Flush bracket No: S3217

Date	Parking ★★★★★	Map Ref: /105\

Start Time	Trig Time

Descent Start Time	Finish Time

Ascent Duration	Descent Duration	Total Time

Total Distance Covered	No. Of Steps

Companions

	Trig Condition ★★★★★

Weather	Difficulty to find ★★★★★

Enjoyment ○○○○○○○○○○

Views ○○○○○○○○○○

Difficulty of walk ○○○○○○○○○○

Highlights

Comments

Zoom in & out on the map using ➕ & ➖
Navigate map using ▲ ◀ ▼ ▶

WINDMILL FARM

Height (m): 140m
OS Grid Reference: ST718290 • OS Grid Ref 10: ST7182129044
Flush bracket No: S5720

Date	Parking ★★★★★	Map Ref: △106

Start Time	Trig Time

Descent Start Time	Finish Time

Ascent Duration	Descent Duration	Total Time

Total Distance Covered	No. Of Steps

Companions

	Trig Condition ★★★★★

Weather	Difficulty to find ★★★★★

Enjoyment ○○○○○○○○○○

Views ○○○○○○○○○○

Difficulty of walk ○○○○○○○○○○

Highlights

Comments

Zoom in & out on the map using ➕ & ➖
Navigate map using ▲ ◀ ▼ ▶

WINDMILL HILL RESR

Height (m): 58m
OS Grid Reference: ST549352 • OS Grid Ref 10: ST5493135273
Flush bracket No: S5757

Date	Parking ★★★★★	Map Ref: /107\

Start Time	Trig Time

Descent Start Time	Finish Time

Ascent Duration	Descent Duration	Total Time

Total Distance Covered	No. Of Steps

Companions

	Trig Condition ★★★★★

Weather	Difficulty to find ★★★★★

Enjoyment ○○○○○○○○○○

Views ○○○○○○○○○○

Difficulty of walk ○○○○○○○○○○

Highlights

Comments

Zoom in & out on the map using ⊞ & ⊟
Navigate map using ▲ ◀ ▼ ▶

WINSFORD HILL

Height (m): 427m
OS Grid Reference: SS876342 • OS Grid Ref 10: SS8769034275
Flush bracket No: S3943

| Date | Parking ★ ★ ★ ★ ★ | Map Ref: △108 |

| Start Time | Trig Time |

| Descent Start Time | Finish Time |

| Ascent Duration | Descent Duration | Total Time |

| Total Distance Covered | No. Of Steps |

Companions

| | Trig Condition ★ ★ ★ ★ ★ |

| Weather | Difficulty to find ★ ★ ★ ★ ★ |

Enjoyment ○ ○ ○ ○ ○ ○ ○ ○ ○ ○

Views ○ ○ ○ ○ ○ ○ ○ ○ ○ ○

Difficulty of walk ○ ○ ○ ○ ○ ○ ○ ○ ○ ○

Highlights

Comments

Zoom in & out on the map using ➕ & ➖
Navigate map using ▲ ◀ ▼ ▶

WITHYPOOL COMMON

Height (m): 428m
OS Grid Reference: SS818350 • OS Grid Ref 10: SS8182935085
Flush bracket No: S5437

Date	Parking ★★★★★	Map Ref: /109\

Start Time		Trig Time

Descent Start Time		Finish Time

Ascent Duration	Descent Duration	Total Time

Total Distance Covered		No. Of Steps

Companions

Trig Condition ★★★★★

Weather — Difficulty to find ★★★★★

Enjoyment ◯◯◯◯◯◯◯◯◯◯

Views ◯◯◯◯◯◯◯◯◯◯

Difficulty of walk ◯◯◯◯◯◯◯◯◯◯

Highlights

Comments

Zoom in & out on the map using ➕ & ➖
Navigate map using ▲ ◀ ▼ ▶

WOODFORD

Height (m): 160m
OS Grid Reference: ST068387 · OS Grid Ref 10: ST0682238736
Flush bracket No: S3749

Date	Parking ★ ★ ★ ★ ★	Map Ref: 110

Start Time	Trig Time

Descent Start Time	Finish Time

Ascent Duration	Descent Duration	Total Time

Total Distance Covered	No. Of Steps

Companions

Trig Condition ★ ★ ★ ★ ★

Weather	Difficulty to find ★ ★ ★ ★ ★

Enjoyment ○ ○ ○ ○ ○ ○ ○ ○ ○ ○

Views ○ ○ ○ ○ ○ ○ ○ ○ ○ ○

Difficulty of walk ○ ○ ○ ○ ○ ○ ○ ○ ○ ○

Highlights

Comments

Zoom in & out on the map using ➕ & ➖
Navigate map using ▲ ◀ ▼ ▶

WRAXALL

Height (m): 137m
OS Grid Reference: ST480726 • OS Grid Ref 10: ST4806272681
Flush bracket No: S3274

Date	Parking ★★★★★	Map Ref: /111\

Start Time	Trig Time

Descent Start Time	Finish Time

Ascent Duration	Descent Duration	Total Time

Total Distance Covered	No. Of Steps

Companions

	Trig Condition ★★★★★

Weather	Difficulty to find ★★★★★

Enjoyment ◯◯◯◯◯◯◯◯◯◯

Views ◯◯◯◯◯◯◯◯◯◯

Difficulty of walk ◯◯◯◯◯◯◯◯◯◯

Highlights

Comments

Zoom in & out on the map using ➕ & ➖
Navigate map using ▲ ◀ ▼ ▶

YANLEY

Height (m): 86m
OS Grid Reference: ST549694 • OS Grid Ref 10: ST5494069427
Flush bracket No: S3262

Date	Parking ★ ★ ★ ★ ★	Map Ref: /112\

Start Time	Trig Time

Descent Start Time	Finish Time

Ascent Duration	Descent Duration	Total Time

Total Distance Covered	No. Of Steps

Companions

Trig Condition ★ ★ ★ ★ ★

Weather | Difficulty to find ★ ★ ★ ★ ★

Enjoyment ◯ ◯ ◯ ◯ ◯ ◯ ◯ ◯ ◯ ◯

Views ◯ ◯ ◯ ◯ ◯ ◯ ◯ ◯ ◯ ◯

Difficulty of walk ◯ ◯ ◯ ◯ ◯ ◯ ◯ ◯ ◯ ◯

Highlights

Comments

Zoom in & out on the map using ➕ & ➖
Navigate map using ▲ ◄ ▼ ►

Equipment Checklist

- ○ ....
- ○ ....
- ○ ....
- ○ ....
- ○ ....
- ○ ....
- ○ ....
- ○ ....
- ○ ....
- ○ ....
- ○ ....
- ○ ....
- ○ ....
- ○ ....
- ○ ....
- ○ ....
- ○ ....
- ○ ....
- ○ ....
- ○ ....
- ○ ....
- ○ ....
- ○ ....
- ○ ....

Ready for your next adventure?

Keeping a log book is a fantastic way of recording your memories - and we have published a number of adventure log books available on Amazon. Simply scan the QR code to find out more!

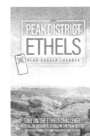

Printed in Great Britain
by Amazon

16992380R00072